PREY IN THE DARK

THE HAUNTING AT THE 32

by

Chris DeFlorio

Additonal cover design by
HKP Productions
Book design and layout by
HKP Productions

Book edit by Tricia Pimental

All photos courtesy of the author

FIRST EDITION

Published by DeFlorio Publishing

ACKNOWLEDGEMENTS

For the Brothers and Sisters at the 32 Precinct
who had my back—on the job and when it
came time to tell this story.

The following people have been invaluable at
different stages of my journey and in bringing
these stories into the world.

Elena Mendez
Keith Pimental
Tricia Pimental

CONTENTS

AUTHOR'S NOTE

Prey in the Dark is told as a dramatized narrative.

While the story is inspired by real environments, emotions, and experiences, it is not a memoir, procedural report, or literal record of events. Dialogue, scenes, timelines, and character interactions have been created, condensed, or reimagined to serve the story rather than document it.

This approach was intentional.

The book was written to be cinematic, immersive, and read in one sitting. Rather than present a step-by-step account, the goal was to capture what it felt like—the tension, fear, uncertainty, and pressure of a case unfolding after midnight.

Any resemblance to actual conversations or events exists in service of the story. Certain scenes, dialogue, and details have been altered, condensed, or combined for narrative purposes and are not intended to represent a literal or complete account of any individual's actions or experiences.

PROLOGUE

This story is part of the *CALLED into DARKNESS* universe. Like the first book, it's told the only honest way it can be told—raw and unfiltered. You are going to run into some bad language in these pages. Not for shock value, not to sound tough, but because that's how cops and first responders actually talk when everything is going sideways. Under pressure, in danger, in the dark—nobody speaks like a choir boy. They speak like human beings trying to survive the moment. If I cleaned up the language, I'd be lying to you. I'd be turning a real encounter into a bedtime story. And this is far from that.

PREY in the DARK is about what happens when the hunter becomes the hunted, when a first responder steps into a situation believing he is the one in control. This isn't superstition. This isn't movie-style horror. It's the moment you realize there's no backup coming, no plan B, no logical explanation to save you.

This account isn't a sermon or a lecture. It's a straight retelling of a night inside a Harlem precinct where things didn't follow the rules, didn't care about experience or training, and pushed me past what I thought I knew about fear. Some moments were humiliating. Some were brutal. All of them were real.

So before you turn the page, remember this:

Sometimes you are the one doing the chasing. And sometimes...you're the prey in the dark.

Chapter 1

PERP AT LARGE

MAY 8 2020

BANG! BANG! BANG!

"Chris, you in there? Chris!"

Chris jumped from his chair as the office door flew open. "Whoa, Andrew, where's the fire, bro?"

"You better come outside in front of the precinct. This rookie is out there telling everybody he just saw a ghost in the bunk room."

Chris looked at Andrew in disbelief. "Is this for real? I'm in the middle of something." But in the back of his mind he knew Andrew wouldn't be screwing around. He had been one of the only cops he could have a serious conversation with about "things that go bump in the night."

It was early afternoon in Manhattan. You can set your watch by the daily blare of car horns, delivery trucks, and ambulance sirens outside the 32 Precinct. Chris pushed open the interior doors with Andrew close behind, arriving on the front steps of the command overlooking West 135th Street.

He saw the cop in question pacing back and forth on the sidewalk, desperately attempting to explain his account to the other uniformed officers. Chris watched from a distance for a minute or two, observing the cop and his actions, not to mention the facial expressions of the other officers. He couldn't hear much of what was being said as the afternoon traffic drowned out the sounds, but he wasn't interested in that yet. Just as a cop will watch body language when interviewing someone accused of a crime, the same holds true when investigating accounts of the supernatural.

Chris saw right away that this rookie must have been telling some kind of story, judging by the reactions. A crowd was beginning to gather around him, but it was not by any means a warmth of emotional support from these hard hitters. The 32 cops were some of the toughest in New York City. Chris stood watching the scene with a smirk on his face.

"What's going on?" Andrew asked.

"He'd have a better audience with a school of sharks in a feeding frenzy."

Chris decided this kid had had enough as he watched him getting beat to hell because of whatever he was sharing. He jogged down the steps and grabbed the rookie's arm, steering him away from the other cops.

"Andrew told me something happened to you upstairs. You want to come tell me? I believe you."

The rookie looked at Chris with relief but also surprise. Chris was known for being a wise-ass, and after the ribbing he'd just gotten from the other guys, he was expecting more of the same.

"Yeah, let's go," he said hastily. As the two walked past the front desk and headed towards the downstairs, the desk sergeant yelled in Chris's direction. "The Admin Lieutenant needs you!"

"Tell her I'll be right up. I'm handling something for her right now."

Chris oversaw maintaining day-to-day responsibilities of the precinct these days. He had only a couple of years until retirement, and being close to fifty years old, he wasn't looking to chase perps half his age at this stage of the game. The two made their way to Chris's office which was in the precinct basement away from any distractions or interruptions.

"Okay, have a seat over there. The first thing I want to do is get the full story." Chris sat down at the desk across from the cop. The room came to a tense standstill as the interview was about to start. Chris pulled out his audio recorder. "You ready?"

"Let's do it," the cop replied.

Following is the transcript from the original audio interview:

CHRIS: It is May 8 2020, 1443 hours at the

32 Precinct. I am here with Officer A [Name withheld] who has been experiencing paranormal activity. Go.

Officer A: My first incident was about a month ago when I finished my first arrest. It was about 4:30 in the morning. I went upstairs to get dressed. The locker room was empty. I was in front of my locker when I felt someone behind me. I turned around and no one was there. I continued getting dressed and when I looked up, I saw the shadow of a person walking down the aisle like ten lockers away by the window. I walked over there to see if anyone was there. No one was there. I heard a locker slam and I spun around. I ran to the area but again, there was no one.

And then last night I had an arrest that ran late. I don't usually stay here, especially after the last incident, but I was wiped out. I laid down on the couch and turned off the lights. Then probably a couple of minutes later, I felt someone bouncing up and down on the couch right next to me. I sat up but didn't see anything. But that couch is not even big enough to fit anyone else. I was really scared but tired enough to go back to sleep.

That's when something grabbed my legs. I tried to get up but I couldn't. I couldn't lift my legs. I broke loose from the grip. And then I heard what sounded like an animal growl. I jumped to my feet and saw the black shadowy figure of a person leaving the room. I couldn't believe what I was seeing.

So, I'm in a group chat with other cops. I texted them and that's when one of my boys told me something happened to him and I wasn't crazy.

Chris paused the recorder. "Wait a minute. Are you telling me that there's another cop at this precinct who had some type of attack?"

"Yeah. I saw him ten minutes ago. You should talk to him, too."

"Okay, let's get him down here."

Following is the transcript of the second interview:

CHRIS: I am here with Officer Michael Feliz. Okay, Mike, tell me about your incident with the paranormal activity in the bunk room.

OFFICER FELIZ: I just finished a collar, and it's around three in the morning. I was in that bunk room in the back. I tried to go to sleep but for the first hour I couldn't...I felt so uneasy. It's like I couldn't sleep. I kept turning to the side because I heard sounds. I don't know what it was. I'm thinking maybe it's the curtains, but I'm like, there's no curtains.

Then I finally started to fall asleep and suddenly I woke up because something pulled my bed forward. I jumped off the bed and pushed it back from the obstructed doorway. I ran outside to see if maybe an officer passed by. So I saw a guy sleeping on the couch. I'm like, I literally just came out here, he couldn't have got to the couch that quick. Now I'm thinking if the officer was messing around with me, if he pulls the bed forward, how will he get out? Because if you pull that bed forward, you know, you won't be able to get out of the room because now you're blocking the door. If anything, he'd push it towards the wall.

I'll tell you, Chris, it was a strong pull. So strong that I could hear the bed drag on the floor. The sound was loud. He or it must have dragged it a few feet at least. I will never go back in that room again.

Chris ended the interview. He had heard enough. Two separate incidents were confirmation enough for him that something evil had befallen the 32 Precinct.

"I appreciate your taking the time to speak to me about this, Mike," Chris said.

"Of course, Bro. I know this stuff is legit. I'm glad someone is going to try to do something about it. Let me know if you want help."

Chris nodded. "Will do."

The officer left the room and Chris just sat in his chair, staring at the wall. He knew this young cop was a tough kid. If he needed help with anyone in the physical realm, Chris would call on Mike without a second thought. But this was different. What was lurking around in the shadows of this spiritual world was much too dangerous to risk bringing in anyone else.

But it wasn't the paranormal events that had him in deep thought right now. It was the fact that he had to explain this to his supervisors. He stood and began to make his way up the stairs shaking his head. *How the hell am I going to explain this one?*

Chapter 2

AND SO IT BEGINS...

Chris stood outside the Admin Lieutenant's office trying to pull his thoughts together. He knew once he walked into that office, he would have no choice but to also reveal the work he does in the dark. Everything was about to change. The torch would be passed to him from the rookie cop as the new precinct nut job. He took a deep breath and pushed open the door.

"Christopher! Where were you? You run when I call you," she yelled as she threw a folder on her desk.

The cop standing next to her turned white. "I'll come back when you're done, Lieu," she said as she hurried out.

This was the room where dreams came to die. The Lieutenant had a reputation for being a hard ass. You usually wouldn't enter that room unless you were summoned, and when that happened, you could expect an unpleasant outcome.

With Chris it was different. The Admin Lieutenant was his direct supervisor. He took care of many petty issues so she wouldn't have to. Because of that, he was given a lot of leeway and unsupervised responsibility. Emma also was very supportive of his ministry expeditions. In 2018 he'd had an opportunity to travel to Africa to help children in a hurting village. She had made the time off possible even without a scheduled vacation. He trusted her and the two respected each other.

"Really?" Chris said, shaking his head.

"That'll make her think twice before asking for a day off," she joked. She leaned back in her chair. "Now, more importantly, you know it's lunch time. Let's go!"

Chris laughed. "Of course, priorities." He walked up to the desk. "Listen, I need to tell you something but hear me out."

"Denied! No day off for you either."

"No, seriously. The only reason I'm bothering you with this is because this rookie is outside telling the whole free world that he was just attacked by a ghost in the bunk room."

Emma blinked. "A what? Stop messing around and get my food. It's all ready to be picked up."

"No, I'm really serious," Chris continued uneasily. "And I got one better for you." Chris knew there was no going back now. *Okay, let's rip off the band-aid.* "I handle this type of stuff."

The Admin stared at him. "What am I, in the twilight zone?"

Before she could continue, her assistant chimed in from her desk. "No, this is real. I have been around this before where I used to live."

Emma threw up her hands. "I don't care if it's ghosts, water leaks, or if the AC isn't working. Just fix it."

Chris turned toward the door, but was stopped before he could break free.

"Oh, and tell Artie to get up here," she said. "Tell him he's getting my food."

He turned to smile at her as he was exiting the office. "Priorities."

Chris started to head upstairs but nearly collided with Artie, his partner since moving from midnight patrol to inside duties. They had become good friends, Frick and Frack of the 32. But even Artie—especially Artie—was left in the dark when it came to Chris's other life. Same with another buddy, Mike. Chris's darker world was not a topic he discussed even with these guys he was so close to.

Artie was a stocky Italian guy with a classic New York personality and a lot of time on the job. Everything was a joke, nothing ever serious, when it came to most things. Chris knew if he told him that he sees ghosts, it would turn into a comedy bit before he finished the first sentence. On the other hand, Chris could give as good as he got.

"Hey buddy, let's hit the gym. I finished the vouchered property," Artie said.

"Yeah, I was about to look for you to see what

time you wanted to go. Right now you'd better get to the Lieu, she has something for you in her office." Chris smiled as he walked away.

He made his way up the four flights of stairs toward the bunk room. The noise of the precinct faded with each flight as he drew nearer to the haunted area, until only the sound of his boots squeaking along the freshly waxed floor could be heard.

At the end of the men's locker room was an area isolated from the main lockers. Chris noticed the door to it was open, as if someone had rushed out in a hurry. The area comprised two rooms. The first, larger, space consisted of an open area with a couple of couches and some additional lockers lining the walls. It was dark inside, but not pitch black. Thin rays of afternoon light pushed between the window shade and the frame.

Past it was the smaller room—the bunk room. This door was always shut. This was the room you only came to sleep in. There were no bulbs in the light fixtures and no windows. It was always nighttime here.

The place was vacant now, as the cop who was trying to get some rest here today had been chased out of the room by something unseen. Chris stood still for a moment. He sensed heaviness in the room, as if the oxygen was being sucked out on purpose. He had felt it before. Most people look for flying furniture or screaming voices to confirm these activities. Those are far from the norm. No, it was the quiet weight that told Chris he wasn't alone.

He took some photos with his iPhone to study later. As he moved nearer to the bunks to get a better view, he felt a sharp pain in the left forearm near his metal plates, that familiar surge. He knew these cops were not overstating their experience. Chris did not react to the pain. He never showed his cards that these things can affect him.

He made his way back to the door to exit the hellish room, making one last turn toward the beds. He knew he was being watched. He knew this would be a battle. He paused before leaving, half smiling to himself. "See you soon," he said quietly, as he pulled the door shut behind him.

The city was in the middle of a mandatory shutdown due to the pandemic that had basically taken the planet hostage. Those who braved the danger and risked public exposure could be seen with their face hidden up to their eyes, having donned masks to protect their respiratory systems from this worldwide epidemic.

An agency like the NYPD never gets shut down, pandemic or not. During the crisis Chris would normally drive to work due to the reduced schedules of the subway system over the past months. Today he found himself using the train, and this day would prove to be far from normal.

Usually he would stand pressed up against the subway doors as the packed, rush hour train rattled through the Manhattan tunnels toward

Penn Station. His sticky boots stuck to spilled soft drinks, helping to stabilize his balance during the rapid winding turns. Chris would look through the window to an adjoining car, watching the commotion as a performer jammed on his saxophone for tips between breaks of noise from the screeching train wheels.

Today he stood quietly in an almost empty car. Often on the way home he thought about his day-to-day duties at work. Not today. Today his mind continued to circle back to what just transpired at the 32. His two worlds had now collided in broad daylight or better put, in the public light. In one world he found comfort. A cop. A father. A husband. A guy with a sense of humor and a respectable job. In this other world he would be something totally different to everyone around him. Different to his family, to other cops, and even to the church. Chris was called to fight in places that most people never speak about. Whether it was because of fear or disbelief, it was something that others preferred to ignore, and Chris had no issues, either, with keeping this in the dark.

Now for the first time those two worlds would exist in the same universe. It had become a reality where anything was now possible in the natural realm as the supernatural showed its ugly face to those who never saw it. Worst of all in Chris's eyes, it placed him right in the middle of the two dimensions. There was no going back now.

The subway had become his sanctuary, a symbol

of his new life underground. An alternate identity hidden beneath the city in the darkened tunnel, unseen by the masses who went about their day. Here he could transform from cop to demonologist without judgment. But today something was different. The darkness felt energized.

A homeless man was Chris's sole traveling companion. He slept, sprawled out on a bench at the far end of the car. Chris felt something was off. The same mechanical noises filled the train's car as on any other day, but it felt eerily silent. A tangible sense of desolation was smothering every sound.

As if the homeless man sensed the same thing, he sat up suddenly on the bench. The two men locked eyes. Chris knew he had seen that same stare before. The train pulled into the next stop and he looked toward the open doors, almost praying for someone to hop on with them. No such luck. The doors slowly shut, then immediately opened again as if something was stuck in them. But there was nothing blocking the door. The banging doors gave way to an odor—something like rotten meat. Chris glanced back toward the strange man.

His stomach dropped as he felt a surge of chills run through his entire body. Unbeknownst to him, the man had silently crept up the car and was now right next to him. As Chris stood near the doors the only thing that separated the two men was a plastic seat barrier at the end of the row. The doors continued to open and shut to what seemed like a rhythmic beat as the two men stared deep into each other's eyes. Chris contemplated jumping off the train. No. Never one to run from something, he refused to break eye contact.

He began to pray silently for God's protection. His breathing increased. There was nowhere to run. He could feel the hate in the man's eyes as his countenance changed. It was if the man was absent and something inhuman had awakened inside of him. The blackness in his eyes were not just a color but an entity. An experience Chris had in Africa years before was his confirmation. This was not something learned in any textbook. This was nothing natural, but something supernatural. What was happening on this train was no accident. No words were needed. This was strategic.

If the eyes were the windows to the soul, then he knew without hesitation what was going on. His new involvement in the precinct demonic activity had not gone unnoticed by the evil that inhabited it. Chris had just been put on notice.

He exited the Long Island Railroad at the Ronkonkoma station and made his way to his car for the last leg of the two-hour daily commute home. On a normal day this would signal the time to breathe. A time to leave work where it belonged—in the city.

But again, this was a far from normal day.

Home was strangely quiet these days now that the kids were away at college. Chris sat at the kitchen table, zoning out to the scraping sound of leftovers hitting the garbage pail as Harmony cleaned up after dinner. She walked over to pick up his plate.

"You barely finished your food. Big lunch with Artie?"

"No. Just a lot on my mind. I can't believe this happened at the precinct. You expect that stuff in some houses or locations people call me about, but it's always something impersonal to me. Now, it didn't just hit home, it exploded."

Harmony stood at the sink, washing dishes. "Tell me again what you were saying about this."

"Well, like I said, this rookie was sleeping in the bunk room and was attacked by something. Something demonic or a spirit. He made a big scene, another cop got me involved, and now I'm The Exorcist," he said with a laugh.

She looked at Chris, shaking her head. "Only you could have this happen around you." As usual Harmony knew the perfect thing to say. Some humor for balance, after he had internalized all of the day's chaos.

"No kidding. It's a far cry from the old days when I would tell stories like most cops. Now I'm coming home with ghost stories." Chris walked over to her to help dry the dishes. "Listen, this could get strange."

"Strange? Really?" Her eyebrows rose. "You mean like appliances-turning-on-by-themselves-in-my-home strange or our-kids-being-terror-ized-on-a-family-vacation strange?

Chris shrugged. "Yeah, I guess those can be

strange. But this is different. If I have to really get involved, people are going to talk. They're gonna know on a bigger scale. Like the whole precinct, big. I just don't know if I'm ready for this."

Harmony looked at Chris. "It's your calling. I witnessed it firsthand in Florida. Do what you have to do and leave the consequences to God." She smiled softly.

That was always the case, and what Chris always needed to hear, to reset his thinking. It was easy to lose sight of at times, but a quick reference to the One in charge could bring instant peace. He smiled back at her.

"Just be careful," she warned. "Stay focused on this thing, not the outside world."

"That's the other issue. There are no outside civilians in these buildings. I'm going alone. I know I did cases before on my own, but this is different. I gotta sneak in somehow and keep this as quiet as possible. What a disaster."

Harmony saw the stress on her husband's face. "Don't do it then. If this is too much for you, just tell them there's nothing you can do. The End."

Harmony loved concluding her points that way. "The End." She made things sound so simple that way. And maybe sometimes they were, but this was not one of those times. Chris always saw the deeper weight of his decisions in this work. This would not be a situation where he could borrow Harmony's quote. Things were already in motion, and he could sense this was about to become an "all hands on deck" event if he didn't shut it down fast.

"Hey Inspector, you wanted to see me?" The Admin Lieutenant walked into her superior's office the following day and smiled warmly.

"What, are we haunted more than normal, I'm hearing?" the Inspector replied, returning her smile.

Relationships between the top staff in the precinct were usually very informal. The Commanding Officer of the 32 was well respected by the ranks under him. He was one of those C.O.'s that come along once in a long, long while.

Emma laughed. "This rookie was beat up by a ghost upstairs."

A sergeant in the room joined the conversation, giving his perspective. "You know, I've seen some weird things here too. Last year when we were organizing a memorial of an officer, I was here talking with Mike, and the officer's picture just fell off the wall."

There was a knock on the door and Officer Pena popped his head into the office. "Oh, sorry, Inspector. I'll come back." The door was almost shut when the C.O. called out to him.

"No, Byron come in here," he yelled back.

The officer did an about face and paused in the doorway.

"Did you hear all about what happened yesterday?" the C.O. asked.

"Yeah, that's what I was coming in to talk to you

about. I just bumped into that kid on the stairwell. He told me everything. I knew that room up there is bad."

"I don't mess with that shit," the Admin Lieutenant chimed in. "Keep that bad Juju away from me," she said backing away with her hands up.

Pena continued. "Remember the last blackout we had in the early 2000s? I slept in the dorm room upstairs, and I tossed and turned all night. I couldn't sleep. I just had an eerie feeling. I kept looking at the door, I kept looking at the window...it was just so uncomfortable. It was such a weird feeling that I couldn't explain, and I never mentioned it to anybody. But I'm telling you, I was not alone in that room."

"Well, I may have a solution," Emma said, laughing. "DeFlorio said he can get rid of it. He's a ghostbuster or something."

"If DeFlorio can do it, what do we have to lose?" Pena said. "Honestly, he is strong in his faith. We talk about our faith all the time. Let him try."

"Okay, get him in here," the Inspector said.

"He's off today," the Lieu said. "I'll call him."

At the fitness center, Chris hopped onto a treadmill. He looked forward to days off when he could get to the gym, his place of peace. It was one of the only times he could shut out all the daily noise, even if only for a short time. The sound of music blasting in the overhead speakers and the mechanical sounds of dozens of dedicated members on their treadmills or

StairMasters became an atmosphere that totally enveloped him. To the average person it might seem distracting, but for those who came here like Chris, it was like church.

He placed his headphones over his ears to listen to his own music playlist, and the outside noise dissipated to the sounds of his own private world. Here Chris could control his thoughts and begin to work out many issues plaguing him throughout the last days. He took a deep breath and increased the speed.

The music stopped suddenly with the sound of an incoming phone call. Chris almost tripped off the treadmill. It was a special ring he assigned to Emma. It never failed to deliver a jolt to his central nervous system.

He grunted. *You gotta be kidding me.* Chris took a second to decide if he would ignore it. He knew two things for sure. One, this wasn't a social call. When he was not there, something would usually stop working or a surprise inspection from an outside department would pop up. The other thing was that Emma was going to stress him out. He sighed, hit the pause button on the treadmill, and answered the call.

"Denied!" he shouted. "Chris can't be reached today, please leave a message."

Emma laughed. "Quit playing," she said. "I'm here with the Inspector."

"Fantastic," he mumbled. "Am I on speaker? Or are you—"

She cut him off as she always did. "No, shut up and listen, get rid of that damn thing."

Confused, his mind wandered. Honestly there were most likely a thousand things to do in that precinct. "Get rid of what?"

"Christopher!" She shouted in her well-known tone. "You know what I mean, get rid of your ghost friend. We want him out!"

Chris stepped off the treadmill in a hurry and walked over to an empty corner of the gym away from everyone. He whispered in a forceful voice. "Are you kidding me? You told the Inspector?" In disbelief, he fired away at her. "How the hell could you tell him? Holy crap!"

"It's fine," she replied smoothly. "We are all on board."

That's all Chris needed to hear. Relief surged through him. He took a deep breath to process what just transpired on the phone call so far. He knew deep down that it didn't matter your status in life, whether position of power or of servant, the devil was no respecter of persons. He figured the Inspector, like so many, had had an encounter in the past. One of Chris's favorite sayings was that most people either had an experience with the supernatural or knew someone who did. Even so, Chris was caught off guard with this one.

"Okay, this is what I can do."

Emma stopped him cold, yelling as though she didn't want to hear any bad news. "I don't want to know. Just get it done, Christopher!"

"Can I just say something then?" he pleaded. "I am not doing this during my regular day tour. You have to get me in there on one of the midnight shifts. I'll do it when no one is around. I don't want anyone to know I'm doing this. We have to get this done quietly before it gets out."

"Okay, whatever you want," she said.

"Today is Friday. I'm thinking early next week, just so I can mentally and spiritually prepare for what I'm going to be dealing with."

"We can talk more on Monday." She hung up.

Chapter 3

YOU CAN RUN BUT YOU CAN'T HIDE

Now that Chris had the green light from his superiors, it was game on. Sure, he was fighting the idea of coming out publicly to his fellow cops as this demon hunter, but that could not overshadow the fact that he was heading into war. He knew what this was all about. It was not like some reality show, ghost hunting for entertainment. This was the longest-running war in history, dating back farther than time itself—the battle for human souls.

There was going to bc much preparation necessary for something of this magnitude. He was going to perform what is known as a minor exorcism. It would be a blessing of a location rather than a person. Most people would think that preparation just means getting the equipment together that he would need to perform the blessing. But it is so much more than that.

When it came to this type of activity, Chris knew that the Bible says it best in Ephesians 6:12:

"For we are not fighting against flesh-and-blood enemies, but against evil rulers and authorities of the unseen world, against mighty powers in this dark world, and against evil spirits in the heavenly places."

It would require spiritual preparation. In his studies he had read of Catholic exorcists fasting for at least three days prior to performing a blessing such as this. It was also very important to confess your sins. It was not a matter of Salvation; our sins were atoned for by Christ at the Cross. This type of confession was to expose what was hidden in the dark. It is very important as it can be disastrous for someone to attempt an exorcism with secret sin.

Chris remembered a story. A group of three or four people were helping an exorcist during a difficult exorcism. This demon was extremely strong and most likely one very high up in the hierarchy. Just when the exorcist was looking victorious in the confrontational stage, the possessed woman looked over at the young man who was helping. As they locked eyes, the possessed woman said to him, "I know where you were last night. Bad boy, Tommy." Tom became rattled. She winked at him, and he ran from the room. The others yelled for Tom, the priest became distracted, and the moment was lost to free the woman.

What the others didn't know was that Tom, who

was married, was having an affair and was out with his mistress last night. No one in that room could have known that. No one human, that is. Any sin not confessed before a ritual such as this is fair game for the demonic to use against a person. It is also one of the signs of a true possession. A demon exhibiting a secret knowledge of hidden things, and it is usually concerning only the people in the room. This was a textbook example for poor Tom and a lesson he would not soon forget.

While the precinct problem was not demonic possession of a person, it was nonetheless demonic activity, and it would be possible to remove it from the bunk room. Chris knew he had to be on his A game.

Chris would have the whole weekend to process all of this and prepare for the ceremony, but tonight it was time to relax. Major League Baseball was still shut down due to COVID, and movies were running dry. As he surfed through streaming films, he let out a sigh of relief. "There you go," he said. He'd found *Jaws*, his go-to movie when all else failed. He sat back with some snacks.

Like clockwork, his Jarvis (Iron Man) text alert went off. *Sir, you have an incoming text message.*

Chris glanced at it and began to laugh as he read the message. *Riggs! What did you get involved in now? Call me.*

"Murtaugh," he said aloud, speaking of his old partner, Reggie, in the plain clothes unit. Chris and Reggie had many adventures to say the least, riding together in an unmarked vehicle during the early 2000s. Chris had been nicknamed Riggs, the crazy one from the *Lethal Weapon* movies. It was a result of the fact that a whole lot more than your typical police work went on than you would think.

On winter nights when things were typically slow, Chris and Reggie would stop by one of the bodegas they frequented and pick up a carton of eggs. They would show up at a call a sector car was responding to. After the radio run or call was finished, they would bombard the police car with eggs as they were about to pull away. That became their calling card.

Unfortunately, it didn't stop there, and Chris found himself in hot water with his own sergeant a couple of times. One thing a sergeant does not appreciate is paperwork. Chris knew that was this supervisor's weak spot.

One time they had received a call for a missing person. The family was very concerned about a young man who they believed may be in trouble and who they had not been able to get in contact with for three days. If something did happen to this man, the sergeant handling the case would be filling out paperwork all night.

As Chris, Reggie, and the sergeant searched the apartment for clues, Chris received a text message from his buddy on the precinct desk that the man was found safe. Seeing an opportunity since the sergeant hadn't received word yet, Chris didn't hesitate.

"Oh man," Chris said. He read a letter on the counter. "To whom it may concern, I'm sorry for leaving you—"

The sergeant cut him off yelling, "Fuck! Are you kidding?"

Chris burst out laughing uncontrollably. Reggie was right behind him as they fed off each other.

"You mess around too much!" yelled his sergeant as he slammed the door on the way out.

Reggie basically inherited the name "Murtaugh," Riggs's partner in the movie. They pretty much gave themselves the names, but they could care less. It was always a good time even if in a bad place.

The last Chris heard was that Reggie, retired for years now due to an injury in the line of duty, was living the life down in Atlanta. The two had not spoken for a while. Chris decided to give him a call and see what that text was all about.

"Murtaugh, what's up bro?" Chris said happily.

"Riiiggs!" Reggie yelled in his usual drawn-out way. "Do I need to come back up there? I hear you're starting shit with ghosts now?" He laughed.

Chris was grinning. "Ah man, I'm not even going to try to explain."

The two worked together before Chris gave his life to the Lord, and Chris was not the same guy with the distorted sense of humor that Reggie used to love. He wasn't sure if he even knew that Chris was so involved in Christian ministry over the last eleven years.

"Let me ask you," Chris said. "How the hell did

you hear about this down there? And even more, how did my name come up?"

"Bro, everyone knows. It's in all the chat groups. They're talking about this kid who was talking some nonsense about a ghost in the precinct. And one of our guys is saying you're a ghostbuster. Damn, Riggs, they're gonna psych you just like in the movie."

"Yeah, I don't think so. It seems like they'd have to psych half the precinct." He paused. "I can't believe all these guys are talking, man. Now the whole precinct knows, not to mention guys who are not even there, like you."

"Well, I got one better for you," Reggie replied. "I read in one of the groups that the news got word of this."

"Are you kidding me?! This is not good. What else did you hear?"

"Nah, that's it. Just the news may show up to the precinct."

"All right man, let me take off. I need to figure this crap out now."

"Okay, Brother. Maybe let Riggs sit this one out huh? Be safe." Reggie hung up.

Chris sat there for a minute. Perfectly frozen, but one thing that was not frozen was his thoughts. His mind racing, sweat began to transpire across his body as he thought about what was happening. *Cops, the news. This is going to blow up.* He jumped to his feet as if he could shatter the invisible ice that kept him confined. "Social media!" he yelled aloud.

It had been almost a year since the fateful trip to Orlando. The trip that changed everything. Since then, he had quietly set up pages on multiple social media platforms with others in this type of unspoken work. It was a beacon to the many who would seek someone to help those suffering from diabolical issues. More than that, Chris always believed these groups offered sanity to people going through these horrific events. For someone to believe when no one else will—that proved to be cathartic for so many in these situations.

But there was now a problem. These groups were part of Chris's other life. A life away from friends, family and most of all, COPS! Plus, now rumors that news reporters are running to this? Chris knew it was only a matter of time before his social media platforms were found out. He had some personal pictures of his equipment and other case findings there.

"He's right," Chris said out loud. "They're going to freaking psych me."

Chris knew that he just lost his period for preparation. Now time was of the essence. He had to move fast if he was going to close this down before it could possibly reach any public outlet. The rookie was running his mouth to anyone who would listen, as Chris remembered. He figured the old telephone game had made its way around the department by now. At this point the story probably was that DeFlorio found a portal to Hell that will decide the fate of the universe.

He needed to move quickly.

It was late on Friday, but Chris knew he had to call Emma at home right now. Even waiting another day could be disastrous for the precinct. As much as Chris worried about his own image, making a laughingstock of his workplace where he spent most of his time needed to be avoided at all costs.

"Emma, I'm sorry to call you so late. We have an emergency," Chris began.

Emma didn't know what Chris was talking about. Occasionally Chris would call about something with his kids and needed time off, but the haunting wasn't even a concern for her on a Friday night. "What's going on?" she responded quickly.

"I just got a call from a cop who used to work at the 32. He said rumors are going around that the news has wind of this and they're coming to the precinct."

Emma was confused. "The news got wind of what?"

"Are you shitting me right now? The ghost and the rookie. And not to mention, someone is telling everyone that I'm the one getting rid of it. God help you if it was you," Chris said, only half joking.

"Not me," she said, laughing. "You think I care enough about this?"

"Well, listen. Next week is not going to work. I need you to get me in tomorrow night. Saturday should be good. The sectors will probably be out all night answering jobs. I could get in and get out quietly."

"You do what you gotta do, I told you. Get rid of it, Christopherrr!" She chuckled again.

Chris heard that all too common tone from her. He desperately wanted to have a serious conversation, but she wasn't concerned? He thought, *I guess I can't blame her. We're having a conversation about ghosts and precinct hauntings on a Friday night.*

"Okay," he said. "Just keep me off the roll call so no one knows I'm coming. I'll just check in with the desk sergeant when I get in and make something up."

Chris hung up and walked over to his blessing kit. As he went to unzip the top of the black duffle bag, he stopped. He was tired. This had been one long day. He put the bag back on his desk. It would be best to start fresh early tomorrow morning after a good night's sleep. He walked toward the bedroom, mumbling under his breath. "Let me get to sleep before someone calls telling me the copy machine is levitating."

Chapter 4

COME OUT, COME OUT, WHEREVER YOU ARE

Harmony rolled over. She stretched out her arm to reach for her husband. The room was softly lit as the early sunrise created a soft glow by the window shades. With her eyes still closed, she could feel the coolness of the empty bed next to her. She quickly opened her eyes. She knew Chris must have been up for a while—but why?

She wondered if the incident at the precinct could affect him this much. As far as she knew he would have the weekend, at least, to process it all and work on a solution. She was completely unaware of the profound event he experienced on the subway or what transpired last night after she turned in. She sat up and looked toward the bedroom door.

Downstairs she slowly pushed open the swinging door to the den. A candle dimly lit the room. Harmony noticed it was almost completely a lake of wax. An empty coffee cup sat next to Chris, telling her that he hadn't gotten much sleep. Immersed in his reading, his head buried in the two open books spread across the coffee table, he didn't notice her enter the room.

"You okay?" she softly asked.

"Ahhh!" Chris shrieked, causing Harmony to jump.

"Sorry." She paused. "You look like you're cramming for a final."

He shook his head. "You don't know how much truth there may be to that."

Harmony looked confused. "What did I miss now? Wait! Don't answer that. I think I'm going to need a cup of coffee first." She reached toward Chris. "Give me your cup, too."

A few minutes later Harmony was settled on the couch, sipping her coffee and contemplating what Chris had just shared about his ride home yesterday. "Okay, so do they expect you to rush in there tonight?"

"No. I told them I needed to. I know that this is bigger than I first thought. Yeah...I need to stop this before everyone hears about it and I have to go into hiding," he joked.

"What do you mean, 'bigger than I first thought'?"

Chris rubbed the back of his neck. "Okay, so I've been up all night studying the Bible, reading up specifically how these demons presented themselves to Jesus or the Apostles when they first encountered them. What most people miss is that these creatures are not babbling idiots, running around attacking people. They are highly intelligent, much more intelligent than the smartest human being on the planet."

Harmony looked at him now with curiosity. "Go on."

"They were part of the hierarchy of Angels at Creation. When God cast them down to the earth, they retained their sense of hierarchy. They still work together, not for good, but to destroy us. They are very strategic."

Harmony broke in. "So you're saying that they work together in a haunting? That they plan attacks for specific reasons?"

"Exactly. They tipped their hand on the subway. I could sense that they were sending me a message to stay away like with the dream before Florida. You can't look for clues as with a police investigation. If you're looking for physical clues in the spiritual world, you'll miss them. But if you use your sixth sense—that spiritual sense many of us have—combined with the discernment of the Holy Spirit, you will see these entities are giving you the clues you need to level the playing field."

"That's amazing." Harmony thought for a minute, then pointed to the other book. "What's that one?"

Chris picked it up. "I forgot I had this. It's *The Art of War* by Sun Tzu. He was a Chinese military commander and strategist from the fifth century B.C. He taught on understanding the tactics of your enemy and defeating him. It's amazing how enlightening this is comparing it to the spiritual warfare we face against the devil. It really compliments the Bible in this area.

"In just one night, I feel much more confident in understanding what I might run into tonight and possible pitfalls I knew nothing about. Some of these pastors in the church just tell you to steamroll in these situations with faith, but have never encountered anything like this or even the devil himself for that matter, which can happen. It's like they just read scriptures without context.

"I mean, what about when the apostles attempted to cast out a demon using only the name of Jesus and their faith but couldn't? Pastors just skip over these scriptures. And not just that. In the same story, Jesus teaches that there are different kinds of demons with different strengths. This is nothing to take lightly. I feel like I'm in for the battle of my life tonight on my own."

Harmony could see Chris was beginning to get himself worked up. Her husband could be very intense when it came to anything he was passionate about. She knew that she had to be his calm voice. He was the cop, she was the caregiver. And honestly, they were right to have her play that role. Who else did he have? She knew how to approach this.

"Okay, honey, take a step back," she said in a gentle voice. Chris was moving into fight or flight mode, and it sure didn't look like flight. "You're already on the road to winning this thing."

"How do you figure?" he asked.

"Well number one, you have God. Don't forget who is in charge. These entities are going in on their own strength. Number two, you discovered their weak spot in one day. You discerned what they were doing on the train and picked it apart this morning. You know what to look for. Use it."

"That's pretty good, coach," he said chuckling. "I taught you well, young Skywalker."

She looked confused. "Young who?"

Chris slowly bit his lower lip. "I can't believe I married a woman who doesn't know *Star Wars*. He stood and smiled, heading to the door. "Come on, let's not ruin a nice moment." First stop was a Catholic church. Chris had worked a handful of cases between his first major run-in at the Florida resort and now, but most were only investigative. The haunting at the 32 would be the first time he was attempting a cleansing with a blessing kit. He had his arsenal, but knew he needed the mandatory blessing of the sacramentals from a priest. Not quite sure of the reception he was going to receive, he made sure to try a church a couple of towns over, just in case.

Struggling to carry the large black duffle bag at his side, he walked into the office area of the church rectory. He gently placed down the heavy bag. Before Chris could speak to the receptionist, the priest in charge made his way over and the two shook hands.

"Good morning, I'm Father Adewale, how can I help you?"

Chris didn't even know how to begin. He had never really shared this part of his life with anyone outside of his very small circle. Chris knew the strict regulations of the Catholic Church. He couldn't imagine what this priest was going to say about a layman like him attempting this ritual.

"Ah...well...do you think I could speak to you in private, Father?" Chris asked timidly.

They made their way to a private room, and Father Adewale promptly seated himself behind the desk, looking at Chris with anticipation and at the oversized black duffle bag with interest. Little did the priest know, today would not be the average day of people coming in to confess this or to ask advice about that.

Chris cleared his throat and jumped in. "Thanks for seeing me, Father. So, I'm a police officer in the City." He hoped his job would get him at least some credibility with the priest before he dropped the bomb on him about what was really going on. First, though, Chris attempted to receive the needed blessing without any explanation. "I brought a bag full of sacraments that I was hoping you wouldn't mind blessing for me," he continued.

Father Adewale smiled. "Of course, my son. Hand them to me one by one and I will pray over them separately."

Chris placed his bag on the desk and opened it as the eager priest stood up. Father Adewale placed his hand on the back of his neck as Chris unzipped the top of the bag. The priest looked inside with awe. There were rows of large jars filled with ingredients, containers of water, crosses, candles, you name it.

"We do encourage people to bless their homes but wow, this is something. May I ask what this is for?" the priest asked curiously.

"A little more than you expected, huh?" Plan A obviously had failed. Chris figured, well, if he couldn't share this with a priest, then who? He smiled. "Why don't you sit down first, Father?"

Chris slowly paced back and forth. He went on to explain all the events over the last few years leading up to this week. Father Adewale sat up in his chair as he became more engaged in Chris's story. Chris, reading his body language, sensed interest, not the instant rejection he was expecting.

"I'll tell you, Father," Chris said. "This was something I never thought of doing or wanted to do. It was as if it found me on that Africa trip."

The room went silent. Father Adewale stared at Chris for a moment, but his thoughts were somewhere else.

"I will share something with you," he began. "I am from Nigeria, and I grew up in a world where spiritual warfare was a daily battle in my village. From an early age I was taught about the enemy. It was not something in a book but a struggle for all of us in ways people wouldn't believe over here. Or honestly, they couldn't let themselves believe, because it would change their comfortable lives.

You are one of the only people I have ever seen since coming to this country who has the mark on them."

"Mark?"

"Yes, you have been chosen to enter this war in a much different arena than most other believers. In my village, we call it the mark, in this country you say, 'called.' You need to understand where you're headed. It's more than blessing a haunted location or simple warfare. It's standing where others throughout the centuries stood as God called them in before you."

Chris sat down. *Now I know how Emma felt when I dropped this on her. Twilight zone, huh?*

"So I'm in a secret society," Chris half joked. He could already feel a bond with Father Adewale.

The priest smiled. "I wouldn't call it that." He walked around to the front of the desk across from Chris and leaned back. He lowered his voice. "Let's just say I know you have been commissioned by God to do what you are doing. No one doing this work has ever wanted it. They were called. You have seen the darkness, I know." He leaned in a little closer.

Chris sat up in his chair. He could see the intensity building in the father's eyes.

"You should be warned. Never forget this. Because you have seen the darkness, they have now seen you. You should not see things as coincidences or random events. When you answered the call in Florida, you entered their radar. Stay alert."

Chris was flooded with emotion. On one hand, he felt vindicated. He was on point with his findings this morning about what he had experienced on the subway. On the other hand, it also confirmed that the warnings in his prophetic dream before his profound experience last summer were not just a dream. *This is real, man.*

Father Adwale sensed the tension. He broke it by giving a little clap of his hands and pushing his weight off the desk before smiling. "Okay, let's go through your war bag."

Chris began to slowly pull out each item one at a time and placed them gently on the table as if each was a loaded weapon to be handled responsibly. First were the two massive glass canisters containing frankincense and salt. Next was a brass censor, and then a container of holy water. That was followed by four religious candles, two representing Saint Michael the Archangel and two representing Mary, the mother of Christ. Chris paused for a moment. Father Adewale raised his hands for prayer.

"Not yet, Father," Chris interrupted. "Just a little more." The two men laughed.

Chris spread out medallions of Saint Benedict and Saint Michael on the table, the objects clattering as metal hit metal. Last, Chris pulled out his most trusted weapon in the spiritual war, a large wooden crucifix with a Saint Benedict medal in the middle. Everything he did in this work was comparable to the tools of the trade as a New York City Police

Officer. This cross was his firearm tonight. The only difference was that it was untested, something he knew was a no-no in any battle. At least he would get the blessing he needed for the sacraments...and maybe a little more than he expected.

Okay, one down. Chris drove toward home, but he knew something was still off. Yes, the tools were blessed and ready to go, but why didn't he feel confident? He let out a slow, unsteady exhale. He still had doubts. It was all happening way too fast for his liking. He was a pragmatic guy. He liked to be fully in charge and now he was forced to rely simply on faith, not his own preparation. His eyes welled up. *I'm just not ready.* He made a quick U-turn and headed for the Long Island Expressway toward Pastor Tommy's.

They had been close friends, meeting in the church almost a decade ago. Chris had always relied on him for his spiritual wisdom, but since the Florida haunting and the support he showed Chris and his family, Pastor Tommy had become the only one he could trust in the church. Chris pulled up to his home and turned off the engine. His hands still gripped the steering wheel, his body lagging behind what his mind knew he needed to do.

Chris approached the front door. Before he could knock, Pastor Tommy opened the door, laughing. "Come in, my friend." He had a laugh that could break the deepest sorrows and reset your mood in seconds. The genuineness and the size of his heart could rock the deceptions of the demonic. One thing the devil hates is a person who is authentic. He hugged Chris, who immediately felt some weight fall from his burdened shoulders as he walked inside the house.

Chris had given the pastor the two-minute drill explanation on the phone on the way over. "Appreciate you making time so fast," he said, his eyes reflecting his exhaustion.

The gleeful atmosphere changed to wartime discussion. "Okay, so what do you need me to do?"

"I need spiritual wisdom. My whole timeline to prepare got cut last night. My mind is all over the place. If I go in there tonight like this, I'm going to make mistakes," Chris said urgently.

Pastor Tommy knew that although he was a pastor, and the one many would come to for prayer and advice, this was Chris's field. Not many pastors had the experiences Chris had in this spiritual realm. Pastor Tommy sat there for a moment. He wanted to choose his words carefully as he looked for wisdom. When he spoke, it was with authority. "Let's just go before the Lord and ask him for everything you need."

The words Chris desperately needed to hear. He had prayed many times for others, but for himself, the words never seemed to carry the same authority. Self-doubt was a dangerous game in this arena, and he needed to be lifted today. The fear of failure was real. In his mind, he had failed at most things he had attempted throughout his life. Missing the mark in professional baseball, the collapse of his earlier marriage, and the destructive relationship with his late father were hurdles he found immovable. But this time it was more than personal failure that concerned him. It was the pressure of the spotlight by the cops. To fall short tonight could put many others at risk.

Chris closed his eyes and bowed his head in a state of confidence. Pastor Tommy's ability and his wisdom to stay in his lane, and to speak in the calling he was given with the power of prayer always made Chris feel as if all of Heaven had his attention. It was powerful. His commanding words shook the room with passion and the promise that the once hopeless mission would be successful. "Yes, yes," Chris exclaimed, as his friend continued to pray.

There was not a pregame football speech by the most seasoned coach that could hold a candle to this prayer. When the pastor closed the prayer out with an "Amen!" it was if Chris could hear the thunderous clap of a huddle break on the last play of a football game. He felt the fire of God race through his veins as he said, "Let's go!"

He had spoken in a low voice but with the fierceness one would expect from a soldier. Chris knew the separation between the love of a Christian towards people and the switch that needed to be turned when going head-to-head with the devil. When he was questioned about this at a church event one day, he simply said,

"I hardly think when God sent the Israelites into battle to wipe out an entire land, they were singing hymns of peace and love." That ended that line of questioning for the rest of the event.

Chris reached for his friend's hand, smiling. "You the man. Thank you so much, needed that."

"I can't imagine what you're facing to be honest," he replied. "I know I can't do this. I'm glad I can help in this way at least."

Chris headed to the door.

"One final thing to remember, brother," Pastor Tommy said.

Chris stopped in his tracks to listen.

"The devil is real, and the devil is strong but He who is in you is stronger than he who is in the world."

He turned to face the pastor. "Then I'll face him."

Chapter 5

GOING DOWN WITH THE DEVIL

Chris slowly pulled into a parking spot behind the precinct. The lot was engulfed in darkness. This was not his usual tour of duty, so anyone spotting him would question his appearance on the premises. He opened the driver's door quietly and looked around for anyone who might be lurking near his car. It was already two hours into the midnight tour. The area was clear. He crept out of the vehicle, leaving his tools for the upcoming battle behind for the moment.

He headed toward the back entrance of the precinct. The pathway was illuminated by the fading full moon, which had been weakening over the past few days. A waning gibbous moon, it was the phase that stirred evil deep in their souls. A time of desperation for the demonic, when the exhausted moon left them exposed. Folklore called it a sign of approaching victory, but Chris knew better. It was also a signal of their last stand. Things were about to heat up.

Chris cut through the alley to make his way to the front door of the precinct. He knew all the ins and outs of the building since taking over the maintenance responsibilities. As he suspected, the curbside parking was free of any police vehicles. This time of early morning historically had the officers' computer screens backlogged with 911 calls. He planned to begin the ritualistic cleansing around two a.m. Most meal breaks back at the precinct didn't even begin until three a.m., but it would not be unusual for them to miss meals on busy nights such as this. Chris would have the freedom to get his own job done without wandering eyes.

Not wanting to check in, he stopped before entering the front of the building and looked up toward the top floor. The room where evil lived. An eerie feeling swallowed him up. Every floor of the four-story building was empty and lifeless except for the men's locker room. The glow from within could be felt down to the sidewalk...or was it all in his head?

Chris proceeded carefully up the worn steps leading into the 149-year-old building. He knew he was entering the most haunted precinct in the city, but there was something more chilling that affected every officer that entered. Directly through the two solid brass doors, a massive wall revealed dozens of officer pictures. Some in old brass frames, while others looked newer. No, it was not an employee of the month display by any means.

When friends of the family who had retired from police work heard Chris was starting his career at the 32, many said he should seek a transfer at the earliest possibility. But Chris remembered one comment in particular. It was one he never forgot, and which he remembered even now as he pushed past the doors. This old timer who lived around the corner had taken him aside. The man's eyes were filled with pain. He had Chris's full attention.

"As soon as you walk in the precinct, salute the desk, walk over to the wall."

Chris thought his choice of words was interesting: "the wall."

"What's on the wall?" he'd asked.

"That's for you to find out for yourself. Never forget it."

The wall consisted of the photos and names of 27 officers who had protected the families of the 32 Precinct throughout the history of the NYPD. These officers had all lost their lives performing their sworn duties. This precinct had more police officers killed in the line of duty than any other in the entire department.

Chris once again looked toward the wall as he walked in to speak to the desk sergeant.

"What are you doing here, man?" the sergeant

asked. "You scamming?" he joked.

Chris began to walk around the desk. The cop on the precinct T.S. phone, at the desk to handle incoming calls for the night, spoke up. "You're here for the exorcism?" she asked with excitement.

Chris froze. Every rehearsed line he'd prepared, straight to hell. "What the hell are you talking about?"

The desk sergeant started to laugh. The night tour seemed to always be left out of the loop. The midnight cop was a different breed. Chris knew this all too well as this was his tour most of his career. Chances are, if you worked on this tour, you wanted it. It was a good place to stay away from all the B.S. throughout the day. You didn't hear about anything, you didn't want to hear about anything. Everyone except this busy bee sitting behind the phones.

"Exorcism?" said the sergeant, laughing again.

Chris glared at the cop. "You're out of your mind," he said to her. "I need to make up some time."

She looked at him, grinning. "Oh right, making up time...on a Saturday night."

"I'll be downstairs if you need me, Sarge." Chris headed to the basement.

On the surface, he played it cool. Underneath... not so cool. *"Son of a bitch,"* and some other colorful words flooded his mind as he took one last glance over his shoulder at the cop. He knew what this was about to become. *We just lost the moon.*

Downstairs, alone in his office, silence. Chris sat there in darkness. He knew the environment upstairs. No lights, no ventilation, no peace. It was not favorable by any means, but Chris was preparing. He began to count aloud. "One, two, three, four," then confirmed, "four seconds." It took four seconds for his eyes to adjust. Every second counted up there with that thing. He was going in alone.

He closed his eyes. He began to pray quietly. Preparation of your surroundings was great, but without God's protection it was pointless. This was a fight where physical strength and might were useless. Spiritual strength was all that mattered. The one piece of training unachievable by human hands.

Chris waited patiently for the two o'clock hour. Time felt immovable. He paced the room like a caged lion waiting for his captors to raise the steel door that separated them. His mind was flooded with emotion. On the one hand, he was ready. He told himself this was not his first rodeo. He has been here before. On the other hand, he couldn't help but think he was way out of his league on this one. Not only could he or others in the precinct get seriously injured, but he was about to be an actor on the grand stage of the department, with a bigger audience than he'd ever intended.

Finally—two a.m.

Chris knew re-entering the precinct through the front with his bags was not an option. He retrieved them from his car under cover of the shadows. One large bag contained his weapons of war. In the other duffle bag was a kit containing a video recorder and tripod. When questioned by Harmony as to why, he'd tilted his head and replied, "Just in case, it will be my last will and testament." She didn't appreciate his humor. She was sitting this out. There was no possible way to bring her into a secure building like this.

Back through the cluttered alley lined with black garbage bags for tomorrow's pick up, he made his way to what looked like a fire escape held together with tie wire and duct tape. He knew the danger of attempting to use this side entrance even without any bags. He put his foot on the first step and was startled by the sound of a long winding creak. More than that, it moved under the weight of his foot.

"Holy shit. Freaking building maintenance." Chris had put over ten work orders for this unit to be repaired. He hesitated a moment, then started again.

As he climbed slowly up to the first landing, he could see through openings in the metal staircase all the way down to the ground. His breathing increased as with each step he thought about what he was getting closer to. It was surreal. *Is this really happening?* The events of the last few days were all leading to this moment.

Suddenly there was a ruckus below. The ground had become a sea of darkness as he ascended higher on the fire escape. There were strange noises. He could faintly see movement. Chris swayed on the stairs, almost pushing through the rotted metal grating on the sides of the railings. He gripped harder and held on tight. *What the hell is that?*

He looked down at the plastic bags below coming to life. A family of unusually large rats were running through them. He sighed. Most people would scream from seeing this alone. That was a common occurrence at this precinct, and most of New York City for that matter. Seeing those little beady-eyed bastards was more welcoming to Chris on this night compared to the ones he was fearing deep down that he would meet soon enough.

When he finally reached the top, he dropped the bags from his strained shoulders. His breathing came in short puffs. Sweat was visible through his blue T-shirt. He needed to regain his composure. He wiped the sweat stinging his eyes. He stood directly in front of the solid metal door out on the fire escape, as if it were a barrier from the danger inside. Once again, he had a fateful decision to make.

Chris paused and turned to look across at the city from his superior position. Bustling nighttime activity there, but here he took in the quietness, a calming peace before an approaching storm just steps away. His thoughts returned to a time only nine months ago when he had faced similar circumstances.

Chris moved the two bags to the side wall on the escape. He aimed his tactical flashlight at the door. He pulled it slowly open as one entering a forbidden room without the permission of its owner. "Here we go again," he said quietly.

He was right about one thing. The patrol units would be occupied running around the precinct tonight. Warm weather was not a friend during these Harlem nights. As a cop coming in for your tour, there would be no rest for the weary. The neighborhoods would turn into their own animal—awake and unpredictable. The streets came alive with hunters and their prey.

"*Shots fired, West 150 and Macombs Place,*" came over the radio.

"*32 John responding!*" shouted one unit.

"*32 David responding!*" from yet another sector.

"*32 Nora to Central*" a midnight cop came across the air.

Central dispatch replied, "*Go ahead Nora.*"

"*This is our job. We are 84 – slow the units down. Will advise.*"

"*10-4 Nora. That's a slow down, all units. Nora, on scene, will advise the units,*" replied Central.

The midnight sectors all arrived at the location within minutes of each other. They gathered outside the cars to look around. Not much was going on in the area. This was a good opportunity for these busy cops to catch a breather. The radio runs had been nonstop for the past thirty minutes.

It was also always a good time to stop for a

smoke. Officer Cerone-Taylor, one of the senior late tour cops, looked over and saw a few of the cops laughing in a group. She was intrigued.

"What's going on now?" she asked.

"CT," one of the cops replied. "That was Valdez on the T.S. She said DeFlorio's here doing that exorcism in the precinct."

Another cop chimed in. "We gotta get back there, I gotta see this."

Oh shit, thought CT. She was close with Chris. He had always looked after her like a big brother since she started her career at the precinct. Many times he would give her his two cents about a guy she was dating, whether she wanted it or not. She usually was not happy with his opinions. But there was also another reason for their bond. She was one of the few who knew about Chris's secret ministry.

A few months back, she had approached him about a spiritual issue of her own. Last Halloween, her daughter had gone to a cemetery with some friends. She pulled out a Ouija board and was looking to have some fun on the national night of ghosts and goblins. The board was a communication device to contact the dead. The danger was that it was promoted as a game you would buy in a store, like Monopoly or Candyland—but that was hardly the case.

The girls placed their hands on the planchette and began to smoothly move their hands in a figure eight motion around the board. One by one, they began to ask questions of the unseen spirit realm. They left feeling disappointed. The cemetery remained as quiet as one would expect a cemetery to be. Silent.

Later that night around three a.m., three knocks in succession were heard at CT's front door. Both she and her daughter awoke. CT looked out the front window. She wasn't opening a door blindly at this hour. What she saw had her take a step back. She rubbed her tired eyes to refocus. Three men stood at the door, their faces hidden by over-sized hoods falling forward.

"Go back to bed," she said quietly to her daughter. "No one is there."

CT waited until they left. She saw them turn in unison and walk away into the darkness. *That's strange,* she thought.

One week later, the same thing happened again, but this time her daughter spotted the shrouded figures. Annoyed, she went to open the door to let them have it. Seeing this, CT pushed the door shut.

"What are you doing?" she scolded. "Are you crazy?"

Squinting her eyes, she looked at her mom. "Really? Relax."

In the past, CT might have reacted the same way as her daughter, but since hearing Chris's experience, she saw things differently now. She confessed to her daughter, "Okay, here it is. Last week when we heard the knocks, the same people showed up looking like that. I didn't want to freak you out."

Her daughter lifted her hand to her mouth. "Mom, that night we used a Ouija board over at the cemetery down the road. We were just screwing around."

"You *what?!*" CT exclaimed. "You know we don't mess with that."

Shaken, her daughter asked, "Do you think something could have followed me home?"

CT wasn't sure, but she knew who to ask. This would be one of Chris's first investigations. He rushed over the next day. She never forgot how he helped her and her daughter.

Now CT looked over at her colleagues. "Listen guys, that's not a good idea."

"Screw that, I'm going," a rookie officer said, laughing.

"I'm telling you, it's dangerous. Plus," she warned, "you're gonna piss him off."

Chris stepped cautiously from the safety of the fire escape into the outer room of the bunk area. With his elbow bent ninety-degrees, flashlight shoulder height in front of him, he cut the darkness in half. His head was swiveling. There was no difference between this and a deep sea diver blinded by the absence of light in the ocean depths. It was difficult to grasp in which direction he was looking until the flashlight beam lit up the walkway.

On his left he saw a dim light at the base of the wooden door that separated this area from the locker room. He couldn't risk being seen there, he would have to set up the equipment right here in the hot zone. It was the only way. He anchored his flashlight—his only lifeline from being swallowed up in the blackness—on the nearby desk.

Chris quickly unzipped the first bag. With precision he pulled out the tripod for the video camera. Extended the legs to be sure to capture the desired height of the room. He placed the camcorder on top and clicked it in. The small area in front of his face glowed as the infrared kicked in. He checked the IR. Adjusted the focus. The camera was his only witness.

As expected, the entire floor was silent, empty of personnel. That was extremely important. In this environment it would be easier to know which sounds were mechanical and which were super-natural. Chris pointed the Camcorder directly at the bunk room door, just a few feet from where he stood. He had an overwhelming feeling the enemy he was here for had slithered back behind that door at his entrance. Waiting. Lurking. An ambush?

His moist hands slipped off the metal zipper as he hastily attempted to open the second bag. He needed to regain his composure. His mind was three steps ahead of his movements. He knew his disadvantages: they could see him, but they were hidden behind a spiritual veil. He took a deep breath. *Focus!* He pulled out the shiny brass censor and softly placed it on the desk.

SLAM!

Chris spun around toward the locker room door. He froze, listening for another sound. He sharpened his eyes as if they could discern the reason for the startling crash. He listened for footsteps out in the hall. *Maybe a cop?* But Chris knew it couldn't be. Deep down he wanted one of the guys to walk through that door and ruin the entire night. Chris would at least have a valid excuse to shut it down and go home. No harm done. But he also couldn't deny that sound. It was not a locker. It was not a cop. The entity was letting Chris know, "I'm here."

He finished emptying the contents of the bag. Lastly he pulled out a new device he was going to try out. An EMF reader. A device designed to detect changes in electromagnetic fields. Many paranormal investigators use this on their expeditions. It was red with a circular shape. Sitting on top was an assortment of LED lights outlining the shape. In the middle was an antenna that could be pulled straight up. If an energy surge approached the antenna, the LED lights would flash colors and a deafening high-pitched beep would alert someone as far as two rooms away. Any layman coming across this device would most likely call the bomb squad. It looked straight out of a sci-fi movie.

Chris grabbed the holy water. He splashed the blessed water in the corners of this outer room—a little pregame preparation. If anything was hiding here, it would stir a reaction. The room remained still.

Okay, this room is not bad at all.

Chris turned carefully to face the bunk room door. His expression said what no words could express. He knew what waited for him was behind that door. It was there that he would go down with the devil.

He walked behind the Camcorder confirming that the recording was still in progress. After what just happened, if there were to be any supernatural activity on the horizon, he wanted it caught on film.

He removed the frankincense and prepared the censor. "Okay, let's see how you do with this," he muttered.

It was time to bring in the big guns. The frankincense would smoke out the entire room. The plan was to scatter the entities as the holy smoke took over the space, a consecration to God Almighty. He fired up the charcoal disc and dropped a few pebbles of resin on top. He closed the lid as the smoke flowed through the vent holes. He wanted to smoke the entire precinct for safety, but this was such a strange circumstance. He knew he was lucky to get this shot. The sleeping quarters were where it had to be done. Jesus had spoken about sending demons into the void, where they looked for someone else to inhabit after being cast out. Chris's plan was to send it directly outside, off the premises.

He stepped to the door. This is where his plain clothes training kicked in. Short tactical steps, one in front of the other. Head up and alert. Holy water and frankincense were his weapons, drawn as he would his firearm on patrol. He pocketed the flashlight for the moment as he reached for the doorknob. The light would give away his position. Little by little he pushed open the door. He lifted his foot to cross the threshold.

Stop! screamed a voice in his head.

He backed up quickly, releasing the weight of the door. The door swiftly closed, slamming in his face. Chris remembered the spring-loaded hinge he had put on months earlier to keep out the light. (Nothing like pissing off an exhausted cop trying to get some rest. That was not an ideal situation.)

He stepped back a minute, pondering his next move. Suddenly it hit him. *"The Art of War,"* he whispered. He paused, remembering Sun Tzu's quote: *"When you surround an army, leave an outlet free."* In other words, don't get trapped in enemy territory. Chris grabbed the broom in the corner and snapped off the handle. He jammed the wood handle into the door frame, wedging it open. If things heated up, he now had a way out.

He entered the room of shadows. The threshold was a barrier between dimensions. He immediately placed the EMF device on one of the lower mattresses before the ritual began. His early warning system of an approaching entity.

It instantly felt like another world, a foreign

land acclimated to the creatures who inhabited it. The air was thick. Oxygen was diminished. Chris trembled. He had just entered the demon's lair. He waved the censor around the outer room first. Like an orchestra conductor waving a baton, he slowly commanded the invisible audience. The mystical smoke began to rise.

What?

He stood there, completely perplexed. Yes, this ritual was relatively new to him, but what he was seeing was not right in any sense. Something un-natural was happening around the bunks right before his eyes. The smoke which freely moved up and about the room seemed to be under attack itself. The frankincense was hitting an imaginary wall. Something was forcing it down, pushing it almost back into the censor.

The laws of nature that govern the rest of us were non-existent here. This wicked creature was openly defying the holy aroma of God. It had obvi-ously staked a claim here.

The deeper he moved into the room, the more his thoughts were scattered. His breathing became irregular. This wasn't Florida. Whatever was here tonight was not looking to hide or retreat. This demon had drawn a line in the sand immediately. *You're in my world now...get ready, boy.*

Downstairs on the first floor it was business as usual for a Saturday night. The lobby was filled with locals. An after hours block party had to be broken up, resulting in multiple arrests. Most of the time they were released with a summons to appear later in court. On a busy night it was more important to have sectors out on the streets backing each other up rather than being tied up inside filling out mounds of paperwork.

The desk phone rang. Whenever it did, it was never a civilian or anyone random. This was an internal line only used for department calls. The desk sergeant answered, his disinterested tone reflecting his boredom. "32 Precinct, how can I help you?" He sat up straight. "Yes, Chief."

"Sergeant, let me ask you a question," the chief said, annoyed. "Is there an exorcism or some crap going on at your precinct right now?"

The sergeant blinked as he tried to hold back a smile. "An exorcism?"

Officer Valdez on the T.S. phone popped her head up and looked at the sergeant.

"Do I sound like I'm playing here, Sergeant?" the chief snapped.

"Uh, you don't. Hold on one second, Chief." He covered the receiver. "Valdez, is this exorcism nonsense for real? I have the chief on the line, and he's asking about it."

"Holy shit, are you kidding me?" She burst out laughing. "Yep, DeFlorio was told to come in and do it. That day tour cop saw some ghost upstairs a few days ago."

The sergeant's shoulders bounced as he tried not to laugh. He uncovered the receiver of the phone.

"Hey, Chief, yeah. There's definitely an exorcism going on here. But it's all being taken care of. It's fine," he said, keeping eye contact with Valdez.

"Of course it is," the chief replied. "Nothing surprises me over there," he muttered. *Click.*

The sergeant stood. He looked toward the rowdy crowd in the lobby, then back at his phone. He sighed, shaking his head. *Is it too late to be a plumber?*

While normal life carried on downstairs, only four flights away Chris was preparing for a battle most humans were never meant for. The battle of his life.

At the command of its new master, the smoke engulfed Chris, chasing him out of the room as he began choking. He scurried back to his bags, and stood over his equipment set up. It had become his turf. His ground. Like a boxer retreating to his corner of the ring after getting pummeled in the first round, Chris looked for safety and encouragement. Only he was all alone up here.

Visibly rattled, he spun about, looking all around. Chris had known this wasn't going to be a walk in the park, but this was insane. He was mystified. The demon seemed to have more control over the workings of the holy essence than he did. He walked over to the door leading into the main locker room. He needed to illuminate some of this area. "Hell with this," he said to the empty room. This was getting out of hand. Without hesitation, he pulled the door open.

Energized by the beam of light now cutting through the dark around him, he glared into the pitch-dark bunk room and saw that the EMF device was still functioning, displaying a solid red indicator light.

He shook his head, puzzled. *Why didn't it go off during the attack?* He inched toward the door to get a better look. Careful not to step over the invisible threshold joining the rooms, he peaked inside. He leaned his upper body forward. Chris slowly reached his left arm inside the forbidden room while gripping the metal frame outside. The silence was deafening.

BEEEEEP!

Chris screamed as the device suddenly went off. He leaped back, running to "his corner." He heard noises coming from just outside the lit area of the main locker room. He crept over, his nerves shot. *A second wave is on the way.*

Whispered sounds and footsteps. His mind fluttered. Was it the demon, a cop, or Buffy the Vampire Slayer, at this point?

Chris hid on the other side of the brick wall separating the two rooms. His eyes were fixed on the beads of sweat from his hair bouncing off the floor in front of him.

The footsteps grew closer.

He peeked around the corner...

Just as he leaned out into the doorway, a shape appeared on the other side. Chris collided shoulder to shoulder and locked eyes with the figure.

He was hit with a crackle of static as a rookie cop clicked the transmit button on his radio.

BEEEEEP! The EMF device erupted again.

Chris jerked. In one motion he broke eye contact with the cop and spun around toward the bunk room.

"Whoa! Sorry, DeFlorio!" the rookie said, chuckling. He jumped back on the radio. "Central, show me 62 at the station."

BEEEEEP!

Chris realized the radio transmissions frequency were setting off the device, not the devil. Angered, he turned and walked up to the cop. "Really?" he spat out.

"I was just talking to dispatch. So, what's going on? This is cool," he said, smiling.

Chris forcefully took hold of his arm like a scolding parent and began dragging him out of the room. "Are you a complete moron?! Get the hell out of here!"

The rookie just grunted, not able to utter a word. Chris pushed him out onto the stairway landing.

The combination of terror and frustration over the last few minutes had culminated in pushing Chris over the top. He stabbed a finger in the rookie's face. "You tell the rest of them down there. Anyone else comes up here, I'm gonna kick their ass!"

The dejected rookie took off down the stairs.

Chris headed back toward the danger zone. He smiled and shook his head, relieved that the tension had subsided. *Fuckin' rookie.*

His cell vibrated and he reached into his pocket. "What's up, CT?"

"Why is a rookie crying in front of the precinct?"

"Really?"

"Nah, I'm playing. But everyone knows what's going on," she added. "My partner is in with a collar, you want me to come up and be lookout by the stairwell?"

"You know what? That's a great idea. I'd appreciate it. One less thing for me to cover. But..." He paused. "I'm being serious here," he warned. "Do not leave the stairwell. This is a bad situation. No matter what you hear, stay where you are."

"You don't have to tell me twice. Be safe."

Chris prepared for the final battle.

Now it was time for religious rites. No intercessory prayer. This was head-to-head confrontation with the beast. He would use the authority given to him through Christ himself, standing in His place. Preparing the environment with the sacraments had failed miserably. Now it was time to bring the thunder.

Chris locked the door to the main locker room behind him. But he opened the fire escape door wide this time. He had still left himself two areas of retreat. Going in this time, provoking the entity with prayer, could dramatically worsen the situation.

He stood in front of the bunk room door once again, half expecting to see two glowing eyes staring back, egging him on. But this is not how they worked. They would be hiding in the shadows, waiting to pounce a second time. Chris lifted the large crucifix toward the opening of the room: Christ on the Cross revealed the inevitability of damnation for demons.

A deadly screech ripped through his body. Fire surged directly to the metal in his forearms like a lased target. Chris used this to expose their hidden locations. His built-in EMF device—the sensation in his arms—told him that they were dangerously close. Hands shaking, he began reading the old Catholic prayer he had printed at home.

The flashlight wedged under his armpit barely illuminated the bouncing paper. His grip was unsteady. His head bobbed up and down, scanning as he read. He was forced into dual roles of infantry soldier and lookout simultaneously.

They were laughing in the darkness. His fear was evident to anyone. He knew that reading the prayers outside the room was pointless. Just another confirmation to the demons of Hell. He was out of his league. He sighed. *Here goes nothing.*

With no more hesitation, Chris stepped into the infested nest. His shoulder caught the broom handle wedging the door.

SLAM!

"No!" he yelled.

Relying on his sense of vision, he swapped positions with crucifix and flashlight. He alternated the beams of light from the page to scanning bunk beds. His voice lacked power. His respiration increased, limiting clarity and volume. Everything was moving too fast for him. *Maybe they were right, maybe I really am in over my head.*

Voice trembling, Chris commanded the ancient entity to reveal itself. On his left the top bunk bed in the far corner shifted loudly. He snapped around, aiming the light at the mattress. The center of the mattress sunk under invisible weight. The springs of the mattress screamed under pressure as if calling out to Chris for help. This was either a colossal creature, or they were just toying with him. Either scenario was disastrous. He rushed over to the bed.

"I command you in the name of—"

He stopped abruptly. The flashlight flickered, then went off. He was blind. He was at their mercy. Chris fought to pull himself together. His earlier preparation proved effective. "One, two, three, four…. Okay, I'm good, I'm good," he said aloud.

His eyes finally adjusted to the darkness. Chris tossed the useless flashlight aside and pointed the crucifix into the blackness. He spun in tight circles as if fending off approaching attacks from every corner of the room. It was his last line of defense—and they were growing in power. He felt them closing in.

SMASH!

Chris winced as the crucifix was forcefully ripped from his hands and thrown to the floor.

He dropped instantly, crawling across the tile, desperately feeling for it.

A scream tore through his mind when his fingers ran over the broken cross. The final sign of defeat. All hope had been lost. Every piece of equipment, every tactical move was easily combated by these creatures.

He slid back into a dark corner. Police instincts were all he had left. The brick wall to his back would guard his six, his blind spot. But this was not a physical battle. The demonic are not contained by man-made materials. Frightened, he pushed off the wall.

The room turned cold. A breeze passed straight through Chris.

"They're too smart, too strong," he breathed, barely able to get the words out. His mind was suddenly flooded with horrific thoughts. *You're worthless, you're outmatched, you have no faith.*

Chris sensed the strategy. The activity moved from the infestation stage to oppression. The spirits were no longer concerned with haunting the room. They were focusing directly on him. He was becoming oppressed.

He knew exactly what came next: possession. If he didn't evacuate now, he risked being taken over. If that happened, he would be doing the dealings of the demons who would inhabit his body.

He stayed low to ground, quickly making his way toward the closed door. He reached it, breathing hard, and reached up to turn the knob.

His hand slipped on the metal. Again and again his hand spun uselessly on the knob as if it had a child safety device on it. In fact, that's how he felt, weak as a child. That's exactly what had become of this night—David versus Goliath.

Finally, one last attempt. The door cracked open. Chris scurried out the door and hopped to the open door to the fire escape. He lay there, half in and half out of the door. He sucked down the fresh air in the same way a thirsty man takes water after a long journey.

Hearing the commotion, CT knocked on the locked door. "Everything good in there?"

Chris couldn't answer. His strength had left him. Everything he had feared had come to fruition. He was overmatched. Then something outside caught his eye—the diminished light of the moon. It was losing its brilliance, its power.

He remembered. *The waning gibbous. That was their last stand. That's all.*

Chris noticed something else. When he looked up toward the moon, he saw the infinite number of stars in the sky as they were brighter, stronger, and more powerful to disperse the darkness. A feeling came over him that all the host of heaven was looking down on him. They were aware of the battle. It was Chris who had forgotten. He had been fighting this entire battle with human hands, with weapons of this world.

As he continued to gaze upward at the night sky, immersed in its majesty, Father Adewale's words began to course through his mind. *Yes, you have been chosen to enter this war in a much different arena than most other believers...in my village, we call it the mark, in this country you say, 'called'...standing where others throughout the centuries stood as God called them in before you...you have been commissioned by God to do what you are doing.*

"Father. All I need is you God, just You," he suddenly cried out. "This is Your battle, Your world. You are God Almighty."

Chris stood on his feet and headed back to the bunk room. His voice grew louder with each affirmation."You are the Creator of Heaven and earth. All things were created by You and for You!" With nothing in his hands this time, he walked toward the closed door. "Visible and invisible," he declared, "whether thrones or dominions or rulers or authorities."

The locker room door to his left shook violently as CT—ignoring his warning—attempted to break in.

Chris stayed laser focused on the victory and continued straight ahead to the lair. He flung open the door leading to the room of his prior defeat. Something was different this time. Fear was replaced by faith. He was given eyes to see and ears to hear. The darkness was replaced by spiritual sight. Nothing was going to touch him.

It was as if he had called down the angels of heaven, invisible to the naked eye but standing in rows like disciplined Roman warriors. They were not visible to him, but they were surely visible to the ancient foe of God. The war in the heavens begun ages ago was ramping up and was the prime time event throughout the universe right now.

Chris led the charge.

The heaviness that once owned the room dispersed around him the way water splits around the bow of a massive cargo ship. The darkness was still present, but it wanted nothing to do with him.

There was something Chris was carrying this time, something that was not made with human hands. A weapon of war that true believers have carried throughout time. A weapon that would shake the gates of Hell.

Making the sign of the cross, Chris shouted,"I command you in the name of Jesus! Depart from this place unclean spirits, satanic forces, and all the legions of Hell!"

A massive shift in energy was felt as the room shook their dimension. It wasn't the words alone. He had spoken them earlier. Now it was the faith behind the words.

"God the Father commands you! he shouted. "Michael the Archangel commands you!"

Chris continued to call out around the room, blessing it and casting out anything and everything ungodly from the other side.

Finally, peace. The room felt different. The

heaviness in the void that had weighed it down was gone. He walked over to the closed bunk room door, and wedged it open one last time. He unlocked the door for CT and plopped down on the chair. His hair was disheveled, his clothes soaked.

She stared at him for a second. "You look like shit."

"You should see the other g—" He caught himself. "You know what? Forget it. You should see the demon."

They laughed.

Chris's phone rang. Harmony. "Hi, honey."

"I wanted to wait to call, I didn't want to bother you."

"No, it's okay. I just finished."

"Oh nice. How did it go?"

Chris paused. He looked at CT and winked.

"Piece of cake."

EPILOGUE

Sometime later, Chris felt human again. He had needed a break, not only from the dark side of the moon, but from the whirlwind he knew was thrashing about the department. The rumors eventually died down around the precinct, as rumors usually do. Things were getting back to normal. He had escaped the battle with only bumps and bruises and had also avoided public humiliation, his greater fear.

Sunday morning. Rami's deli—his usual spot—for some family breakfast. As Rami rang up breakfast, Chris picked up a copy of The Daily News and dropped it onto the counter. He froze. All the blood left his face. He slowly lifted his eyes and looked at Rami.

Rami stared back at him, mouth wide, then turning into a grin. He pointed at the front page and then at Chris.

"You!"

PHOTO ALBUM

My exact view walking up the fire escape that night, leading to the bunkroom.

Actual still photo from the video of me reading the prayers during the minor exorcism

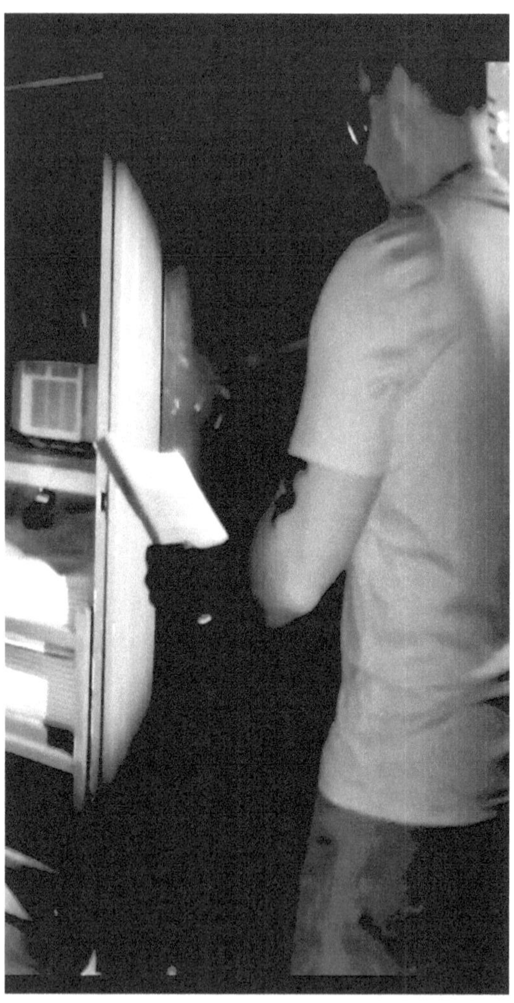

An unknown cop had some fun - Ghostbuster photo in the 32 precinct window after the news spread about the incident.

Sunday Daily News - The day the World found out!

Mock wanted poster displayed through out the precinct by an unknown cop having some more fun.

| POLICE DEPARTMENT CITY OF NEW YORK | DETECTIVE BUREAU Wanted Flyer # 57021567 | POLICE DEPARTMENT CITY OF NEW YORK |

INFORMATION NEEDED FOR ASSAULT

PERPETRATOR - PROBABLE CAUSE TO ARREST

UNKNOWN UNKNOWN / MALE / BLACK

ON 5/8/20 AT APPROXIMATELY 1200 HOURS THE ABOVE PHOTOGRAPHED SUBJECT IS WANTED IN REGARDS TO JOSTLING UMOS INSIDE OF THE 32 PRECINCT. THE 32 PRECINCT DETECTIVE SQUAD IS ENDEAVORING TO IDENTIFY THE ABOVE SUBJECT.

Anyone with information regarding the above subject

Investigator: 32 PDU
Command Assigned: 32 PRECINCT
Case#   1   Complaint Report # PENDING

Clockwise - Artie, me, and Byron.

Me and CT rocking the spectacles at the
Optical Enhancement Unit.

AFTERWORD

Some readers may finish this book wondering why there was not a clear understanding of why this happened. The answer is simple. This wasn't fiction. It was a true event. And the truth is that sometimes there are no answers to why or how. Real life does not follow a script. We would love to hear it was a ritual gone wrong, a curse, a tragic death—something perfectly clear. We want that aha moment where we "get it" and it's all neatly wrapped up.

In this case, the origin was never discovered. That isn't a missing chapter. It's the cold reality of spiritual warfare.

Not knowing why can be its own trauma. It can leave you searching for a meaning that may never reveal itself. Sometimes that uncertainty is part of the enemy's strategy.

People often ask how these things happen at all. The best answer I can give, especially in this situation, is that evil hates good. Its purpose is to kill, steal, and destroy. When I talk about "good," I am not talking about it from the perspective of human goodness. I mean cosmic good. The perfect goodness that rules the universe in all things. The measure of that goodness is God.

What I tried to relate in this story is that what I was part of was much bigger than me or an inciting event. This war has existed long before our world existed. Long before recorded time, Lucifer and a third of the angels rebelled against God. Scripture doesn't give us all the details—some things are not for us to know—but one thing is clear. Since their fall, their mission has been to destroy mankind. This may be their fight, and the conflict we have been born into, but some of us are called into it directly.

What happened inside that bunk room was a perfect example. Sometimes there is no inciting incident. No bread crumb trail. No victory lap. Sometimes there is no clear-cut explanation or complete victory. Sometimes the battle is won just enough for you to prepare to fight another day. But the impact is undeniable.

This was not your typical detective story. It was a collision of good versus evil, faith versus fear. If there is something to take from this, it's that we all face a version of that room. Maybe it doesn't appear in the form I witnessed that night in Harlem. Maybe yours is family tragedy, an unrecoverable financial loss, a medical diagnosis and/or the heavy burden of wearing a gun and badge. Whatever it is, fear is always the enemy's move, and, as we know from Sun Tzu, it's key to know your enemy.

The main takeaway is that fear will never lead to answers, but only to an endless sea of questions. I fell into this trap myself. It was only when I realized the truth that I found the strength to fight. God created all things. God rules all things. And all I truly needed was Him. That's when peace came. And with it came victory.

So, I ask you, what is your battle? What is defeating you right now? Some battles don't begin with a valid reason. They begin with an attack. With an onslaught. Society tells you to stand your ground and fight with all your might. Yes, that matters. But if you want real victory when hell sends its forces into your life, remember this: Heaven's armies stand ready. Your Father in Heaven stands ready.

All you have to do is ask.

ABOUT THE AUTHOR

Chris DeFlorio was a Nationally Certified Paramedic during the 1990s while running an ambulance in the busy South Bronx for the New York City Fire Department. After he moved to the New York City Police Department in 2003, he spent years in the plain clothes unit as a cop at the dangerous 32nd Precinct in Harlem. There he experienced every kind of evil while studying the crime habits of the city's worst and most violent offenders.

He is a Christian who has worked in ministry for more than fifteen years ranging from evangelism to caring for the homeless throughout New York City to missionary work in Africa.

DeFlorio has been featured in *It's Coming,* an international documentary, and he has been interviewed for dozens of articles spanning topics from hauntings to visionary serial killers like Ted Bundy and Lori Vallow.

Along with his wife, Chris now combines his first responder skills acquired over twenty-five years of experience with their faith as they travel the country investigating and helping families with demonic issues infesting their lives.

Website: www.chrisdeflorio.com